MW01485681

Presented to:

Never Forget The Difference You've Made

Made in the USA
Las Vegas, NV
03 August 2021

27534595R00061